Who's Raising Our
Children

Who's Raising Our
Children

Jan D Snead

Gotham Books

30 N Gould St.
Ste. 20820, Sheridan, WY 82801
https://gothambooksinc.com/

Phone: 1 (307) 464-7800

© 2025 *Jan D Snead*. All rights reserved.

No part of this book may be reproduced, stored in a retrieval system, or transmitted by any means without the written permission of the author.

Published by Gotham Books (June 3, 2025)

ISBN: 979-8-3485-1782-3 (P)
ISBN: 979-8-3485-1783-0 (E)

Because of the dynamic nature of the Internet, any web addresses or links contained in this book may have changed since publication and may no longer be valid.

The views expressed in this work are solely those of the author and do not necessarily reflect the views of the publisher, and the publisher hereby disclaims any responsibility for them.

TABLE *of* CONTENTS

INTRODUCTION vii
PARENTING 1
   Making the Right Call 1
   It May Be Small, but It Matters 4
   Parenting and the Political Arena Don't Mix 5
   It Takes a Village 6
   Too Much Information (TMI) 7
OUR CHILDREN ARE CONFUSED 8
   Adults Are Supposed to Know Better 9
   The Wrong of It All 10
   Popcorn Generation 12
   Justice Is Unjust! 12
   Morally Challenged 16
CHARLIE BROWN SYNDROME 20
   Psychiatrists 23
   Adults, Your Behaviors Are Being Watched 24
   Parents Should Strive to Be Much More 25
HANGING IN THE BALANCE 27
   If You Think You Have a Right 30
   America Is Sick 31
   Everything Has a Price 32
THE CREDIT AND THE BLAME 34
   Accountability 35

  Our Judicial System 36
  The Grass Is Always Greener 38
WE SHOULD LEAD BY EXAMPLE 41
  Pay It Forward 45
  Our Fathers Are AWOL 46
  Charitable Contributors 47
THE HOUSE THAT JACK BUILT 49
SUMMARY 54
MESSAGE TO PARENTS 57
MESSAGE TO THE CHILDREN 59
TO THE NEWTOWN COMMUNITY 61
TO THE PARENTS OF TRAYVON MARTIN 62

INTRODUCTION

There is not a more rewarding job than parenting. It's tough, but the realization that we actually get to mold the lives of our future brings a great deal of gratification. This fact was not lost on me. I took my role as a parent seriously, and I was creative in implementation of said role.

When my children were young, I would play a game with them. I waited until they were dressed for school, and then I'd ask them what their clothes said about them. One day, my eldest child came out of her room wearing what I can only describe as a clown outfit. I asked her what look she was going for. She said, "It's the style!"

I knew immediately that her thought process had to change. It was important to me that my children understood that fads come and go—but individuality never does.

As parents, in our attempts to prevent our children from being ostracized, we cause them to become victims of peer pressure. We want our children to fit in, so we allow them to go with the crowd. We don't limit negative exposure that can affect their lives. One such example is television. There was a show called *Pretty Little Liars*, and another called *The Lying Game*. If the producers of these shows were my children, I would ask them what they were trying to convey. I'm hard-pressed to understand why such shows even exist. What message is communicated to the watcher of these programs—who, more often than not, are teens? Parents who allow such shows to be viewed by their children convince themselves that they're harmless, but in reality, they know how impressionable children are.

Television doesn't only influence children; for adults, reality shows dominate our television programming, and they are an atrocity. They strip the common decency of people who are supposed to be authoritative figures in our society. *Big Brother, Survivor, Basketball Wives,* and *The Sisterhood* demean, debase, and degrade. Nothing is sacred, and no one is exempt; however, the fault is not only on the producers. The participants must bear some responsibility for their parts in this disgrace of morality. We air our dirty laundry on these shows and then wonder why our children text, sext, Facebook, and TikTok too much information.

This error in judgment doesn't stop with the television lineup. Try watching an advertisement, the sexual undertones are such that the purpose of the ad is lost. It would be great to see a commercial about the product and not about what's eating it, who's lying on top of it, or the promise of some unfulfilled desire if you purchase it. In addition to trash congesting our airways, games for Xbox, Nintendo, and various other game consoles are loaded with inappropriate content. Sadly enough, children don't buy these games—parents do! If parents are not concerned about what their children are absorbing, they will be responsible for the destruction of our youth.

The most amazing behavior though, by far, is that there is only one restriction to what enters our children's hearts, bedrooms, and their person. Jesus Christ is forbidden from entering our homes, our schools, our courthouses, and our lives. What did Jesus do so badly that he should be forbidden to enter any aspect of our world? He taught us to love our enemies, bless those who curse us, do good to those who hate us, and pray for those who spitefully use and persecute us.

I'm amazed that the separation of church and state only applies to the church. The military has its own police, lawyers, and judicial system. Whenever there is an indiscretion within that organization, civilian laws have no jurisdiction in their affairs. When it comes to the church deciding to settle matters according to the laws of the Bible, it is subject to secular law. The church has lawyers, doctors, judges, and guidelines for conduct, but when executed, it is subject to the laws of the land.

America has confined Jesus to the church, and he only matters when disaster strikes. Suddenly there is standing room only in our churches, our synagogues, and our temples, but as soon as the danger is forgotten, so is God! In reference to our service to God, do we or don't we, can we or can't we, should we or shouldn't we?

These mixed messages confuse our kids because we are wavering on what we know is right. We must stand firm about the fact that without God in our lives and failing to live a good and acceptable moral standard, all that we do is in vain—and destruction is eminent. We find it easy to stand for immorality. We dress it up in an attempt to change its appearance instead of taking a moral position and setting quality standards for our children. Weakness breeds weakness, which is apparent in the mindless disregard of our government and laws toward parents. Jesus poses no threat to our humanity; the greatest threat is instituted by our government and its attempts to redefine the structure of the family.

We should have the mindset of Paul, a follower of Jesus. He said, "Finally, my brothers, whatsoever things are true, whatsoever things are honest, whatsoever things are just, whatsoever things are pure, whatsoever things are lovely, whatsoever things are of good report, if there be any virtue, think on these things!"

PARENTING

There was a time that when someone said, "I am a parent," it was assumed a pregnancy had occurred that resulted in a birth. Now with infertility issues, becoming a parent can happen through adoption, in vitro fertilization, and surrogacy. The act of parenting is the same regardless of how one becomes a parent, but what is a parent? It's more than the act of producing offspring. Parenting is an institution. It is the art of taking life's experiences and utilizing them as tools to become teachers of the next generation.

Experiences shape who we become. They are not intended to break our spirits; they are meant to build character. Somehow, in spite of all that we could gain from life's lessons, we use them to excuse bad decisions and immoral behavior.

Making the Right Call

Do we consider how an impending birth will change our lives while our babies grow in our bodies or the responsibility required to raise a good person? It is my belief that carrying a child for up to forty weeks creates a bond between mother and child. Nothing can prepare us for the love we experience when we see our babies for the first time. We are so amazed as we watch them take on their own little personalities. Everything they do has a sense of wonder and awe, but it is important to set boundaries early on; in doing so, we establish respect.

I want to believe that having a child means more than dressing them up and showing them off. Unfortunately, many behaviors seem to point to the contrary. Poor parenting has produced a nation of obese, unhealthy, and mentally unstable children. There are bullies and socially withdrawn children. We have children who are being diagnosed earlier and earlier with depression, bipolar disorders, schizophrenia, and disorder like stemming or shadowing which is often found in children with Autism.

The experts would have us believe that these are genetic disorders, but where do they really originate? What role does environment, diet, self-esteem, and influence play in these disorders? Is it possible that parental intervention could influence human behavior?

When we fail to execute our role as parents, our children suffer—and so does the world. We have parents who can't figure out that eating fast food every day is not healthy or responsible. It's not difficult to consider cause and effect. Foods full of sugar and sodium create the need for bigger clothes and more medical appointments.

It's okay to say no to your children. For some reason, many have bought into the idea that raising children is easier if you avoid confrontation. Many parents think that giving children as much leeway as possible until they reach the age of eighteen is all that is required to complete the job. This kind of thinking unleashes unprepared adults into society with a false sense of competence. It doesn't take much effort to sum up the kind of adults we are producing.

Experts say that children develop much of their capacity for learning in the first three years of life. Those are the years that anger, unhappiness, disagreements, and temper tantrums are to be expected. Living at home simulates the real world. Tell them when they're underperforming and when you know they can do better. Correct them when they are wrong—and use chastisement when needed. I don't know who thought it was a good idea to stop telling our kids that certain behaviors are wrong. Who decided we should ask them if there was a better way they could have handled a particular situation? There are serious challenges when raising children, but parents are supposed to provide the necessary stability, morality, integrity, and teaching to nurture humanity for the next leg of our aging world's journey.

It is important to realize that employers, fellow employees, and many who may come into contact with young adults could care less if he or she is uncomfortable with authority. As young adults, they are expected to perform certain duties and assignments. Everyone may cower in fear when a child throws a temper tantrum at home, but in the real world, that behavior will get you fired with a police escort. You're not doing your children any favors when respect for authority, proper behavior, and emotional responses are not taught or enforced. Long before these children become adults, the signs are visible to adults entrusted with their care and education; daycare providers and schoolteachers know how these behaviors affect future accomplishments.

Allowing children to control the home environment lures them into a false sense of empowerment. The Columbine shootings and the Oklahoma City bombing show what happens when questionable behavior is unchecked. We see desperation, depression, despair, and fatal results in the form of retaliatory actions. If you've ever looked into the eyes of a person who has lost all hope, you'll admit there is little more frightening. A person who feels he or she has nothing to lose is dangerous!

These people were not always desperate. There are many phases from contentment to desperation and our role as parents, mentors, and counselors is to be in a place to intervene. Perhaps if we had been fulfilling our roles, some of the chaos of late could have been deterred. I am confident that we can produce morally based, integrity-filled, conscious-driven adults with the proper structure. Let me break it to you gently: whether it's your child or someone else's child, you never stop parenting!

Having said that, I believe some parents should have their parental privileges revoked. What are parents who believe it is okay to give birth in front of their children thinking? Blood and travail are nothing to relish! Let me put this in perspective. Consider that your children think of you as their everything, the only god they know until they seek a higher being for themselves.

Most children believe their parents are invincible, strong, wise, and dependable. Children know their parents have their backs in all of life's challenges. If the object of admiration exposes herself—partially clothed, legs in the air, in laborious exertion, sweating and crying in pain to bring forth life—the tumultuous emotions, fears, and insecurities evoked for a child could be irreversible. Once that event is seared into a child's memory, it cannot be unseen or unheard. Regardless to how wonderful you think the miracle of birth is, you have no business exposing your children to it!

Other parents think that being the perfect parent means creating an environment of fantasy. They believe that children thrive when they choose what they want to be. They create gender-free homes! Moms, teach your girls to be true women. Dads, teach your boys to be real men. It is insane to allow any toddler, teen, or adolescent to chart the course of his or her life. They have no idea about the consequences or repercussions of such decisions.

The role of parenting is not where you let the fear of exclusion influence your judgment of right and wrong. We're so concerned with how people will judge us if we dare to act according to our design. Do the job that was entrusted to you as a parent, counselor, clergy member, neighbor, or friend. At the end of the day, if you had the opportunity to make a difference and didn't, there is enough blame to be shared by all.

It May Be Small, but It Matters

As a parent, you choose your battles. Some may not seem worthy of addressing because of the sheer simplicity of the matter. For example, it is not okay for your children to call you by your first name. It shows lack of respect for the authoritative figure. The respect of a parent is the beginning of knowledge, but it's not owed just because you are the parent. It must be earned. That task will be made all the more difficult when the desire for your child's happiness crosses the forbidden boundaries, such as providing alcoholic beverages to them.

I am perplexed by the idea that some parents justify purchasing alcoholic beverages for their children. These parents say, "They are going to do it anyway; I might as well provide a controlled environment in which they can do so." Any parent worth their grit knows that nothing good can come of such a decision. Once that permission is given, regardless of your little speech about only doing it at home, an adolescent thinks he or she has all the answers and can outwit you.

Are you really naïve enough to think that once tried, it won't be anywhere else? Get this through your head: it is not possible to be a parent and your child's friend. Your child is not your hangout buddy. They don't need a parent who is a friend; they need a parent who is a parent. When you cloud the lines between parent and friend, you lose the advantage of authority. You lose the respect due to you as a parent. Parents, exercise common sense and make the right call!

Parenting and the Political Arena Don't Mix

Since many parents have abandoned the institution of parenting, politicians are filling the void. Former New York mayor Bloomberg tried to pass a law against large sugary drinks. McDonald's has been sued for making children fat, and the food industry has had to rethink how food is processed. Someone needs to inform our legislators that rearing children is not their job.

It's long been said that if you're not a part of the solution, you're part of the problem. Much of the interference into raising children by politicians is more destructive than constructive. Parents are finding themselves in court for disciplining their children. How does punishing parents for discipline help anyone? How does overriding chastity as opposed to distribution of condoms move us toward accountability? How does making Plan B available to fifteen-year-olds make sense when Plan A should have been practicing abstinence?

When the driving force behind passing legislation becomes a popularity contest, no one wins. If it's true that we lead by example, we have a serious problem. I see no way that a foundation of accountability, morality, integrity, or responsibility can be gained with the virtual landslide of impropriety!

It Takes a Village

It really does take a village to raise a child, but the village never included politicians and psychologists. When a parent senses danger on the horizon, the word is sent out to all parties to coordinate a plan of attack in preparation for the unseen force.

The members of the village are no longer allowed to make the necessary decisions for a productive society. There is a great deal of stigma attached to parents who read their children's diaries or enter their bedrooms without asking or knocking because it infringes upon their right to privacy. Parents are made the enemy, and athletes and movie stars become role models. How can someone we only see in movies, on a basketball court, singing a favorite song, or swinging a bat, racquet, or golf club replace living, breathing, interactive people? After all, we really know nothing about them except what we see on TV, which has been produced, directed, and edited.

In Lance Armstrong's interview with Oprah Winfrey, he said he considered doping as much a part of the sport as pumping up his tires or putting water in his bottle. This man—the winner of seven Tour de France titles and a cancer survivor—was reduced to a liar and a cheat. How can someone of this caliber have a gray spot in a world of black and white?

He was a role model for many people—and not just children. Clearly, he felt entitled to do whatever he wanted, and he communicated that message in his interview as matter-of-factly as someone talking about shopping for new shoes. He was stripped of his medals and titles, threatened with lawsuits, and asked to provide information about the doping allegations. He was not, however, required to make emotional or moral restitution for his blatant deceit. The conflicts and impressions made on our children by the adults who are supposed to be held in such high esteem are derailing positive efforts.

Too Much Information (TMI)

The information reported through our media about Lance's doping should never have been divulged in such detail. The media has become so busy trying to get exclusive interviews and be the first to lead with breaking news that they don't even stop to ask themselves if they should. They reveal too much.

By the time the Armstrong story was exhausted, there was nothing left to speculate about. What he did, how he did it, why he did it, and where he did it was reported in such detail that, if some misguided child who was longing to fit in and needed an edge to make him popular had listened to all the reporters—who were trying to outdo each other by revealing information to the point of endangerment—he would have been armed with enough information to have repeated some form of Mr. Armstrong's actions.

This was also true of the Boston Massachusetts tragedy. Every night and all day, there was report after report of every minute detail—from where the brothers learned to build the bomb and the remote used to detonate it to where they purchased the fireworks to get the black powder for the explosive devices. No one practices censorship anymore. Does anybody understand the meaning of *enough?*

OUR CHILDREN ARE CONFUSED

We let our children down when we don't exercise parental control. It is an act of child endangerment to allow them to use social media and the World Wide Web without teaching them the responsibility of such a privilege. No one explained that everything they post leaves them vulnerable to the world of virtual opinion and gives complete strangers power over them.

Children don't understand that what they post on social media can follow them for the rest of their lives. These posts can prevent them from getting into good colleges or attaining good jobs. They are exposed to predators and are influenced by people who should have no effect upon their lives.

Things as simple as dressing themselves with a discerning eye or viewing themselves through the eyes of a potential employee are beyond their comprehension during the adolescent years. Our kids are walking around with their pants under their behinds, showing their underwear, and they don't even know why they do it or what purpose it serves. Their behavior is disrespectful, and their language is atrocious. If you've ever attended a high school sporting event and listened as you try to watch the game, you've discovered that the attendees are such a distraction that you can't enjoy the game. There's no respect for the adults in their presence. Where are the parents of these foul-mouthed adolescents?

Adults Are Supposed to Know Better

A father and mother are necessary to create a loving and stable environment. However, with the conduct lately of men and women—and mothers and fathers—it's no wonder that our children are diagnosed with conditions that used to be present mostly in adults.

Nowadays we can't send our children to school, church, a friend's house, or even a relative's home without the fear that they could be abducted, raped, assaulted, or murdered. Many of the adults necessary for our children's growth and development are complete strangers, but we trust them because of the positions they hold in society or in our lives. How much can we really know about a person? How many times have we seen horrific scenes on television of mass shootings or acid being thrown into the faces of women or men by a jilted ex? The interviews that follow make you wonder if these people had multiple personalities or if friends and family members really knew them. Imagine the kinds of people who perpetrate such heinous acts being placed in positions near our children.

People who are supposed to be providing leadership and guidance for our children can't be trusted. Doctors, lawyers, teachers, reverends, coaches, school bus drivers, government officials, police officers, and judges have all made scandalous headlines in the past. What is wrong with adults? It is a frightening thought that the people we are entrusting our children to could be responsible for their demise.

The NRA has stooped to an all-time low—at the expense of children's lives. They selfishly bicker over what is important to them without weighing the impact of such foolish ideals on the ill-prepared next generation. No matter how many innocent little faces we see killed as a result of gun violence, the NRA will not compromise. Instead, they selfishly cite the right to bear arms, knowing that firearms that can empty a 30 round magazine in 2.25 seconds means the possibility of hundreds of innocent lives can be taken in a matter of seconds. They thoughtlessly put their own desires before the value of innocent blood. Gun advocates prey on the ignorance of people who believe that the gun control laws we're trying to pass will rob us of our rights. It is the right of every American to bear arms, but these types of assault weapons serves one purpose: to take human lives. We should be intelligent enough to recognize this ploy for the baseless strategy it is: a fear tactic meant to drum up support in favor of bigger and more powerful guns, regardless of the number of children dying.

The Wrong of It All

America is in a perpetual moral landslide. It is sad that we don't even know it. We are calling wrong "right" and right "opinion."

Take a virtual walk with me as we attempt to decipher this moral landslide.

Say you are a young woman who has successfully completed high school and is paying your way through college. You want to get an apartment to launch your independence, and you begin apartment hunting. You know that your income is limited, but you can make it with a roommate. Your search starts with low-income apartments. Everywhere you go, they ask how many children you have. When you say none, they say, "Sorry. You must have at least one child to live here."

For baby mamas, there are programs such as WIC, food stamps, Section 8 housing, childcare assistance, and help finding employment. If you have a deadbeat baby daddy, you get a welfare check. What is right about that? There are no programs for those who are trying to better themselves; everything goes to those who are not.

It's not rocket science to require everyone to get a job. There is certainly nothing wrong with our country wanting to help our own people, but why not subsidize income with state assistance? It should not be an all-or-nothing policy. When going to social services for assistance, they should be required to bring a paycheck stub. Calculate the cost of childcare, basic utilities, food, and necessary essentials (such as toiletries) and supplement the income. No one earning less than $20,000 annually should have to pay income taxes. With the cost of living, who can live on that? This proposal would improve our jobs report, save the states money, and stop enabling lazy young adults with no aspirations to better themselves.

Many of our adolescence are computer savvy, but they live in a virtual world when it comes to building a life. Their career choices are not based on reality. They think anyone can be a professional athlete, movie star, or recording artist. They don't realize that building a financial future takes work and education. It doesn't help that our world of entertainment paints a mythical picture of success. It's easy to understand why kids don't believe that it takes hard work to attain a good living. Paris Hilton, Kim Kardashian, and Farrah Abraham became famous with the assistance of sex tapes. Apparently, finding yourself in a compromising position is big business. When big paydays and movie-star status can be achieved in this matter, what is the incentive to strive for excellence? Clearly, the greatest rewards are given to those who are ethically challenged.

Hard work is not easy, and the pay isn't as good. There is no market for integrity. I listened as Farrah Abraham attempted to explain to an *Entertainment Tonight* reporter why she hired a porn star to have sex with her. It made absolutely no sense, and listening to her confirmed for me that she lacks common sense. She's a teen mom, the author of a *New York Times* bestseller, and she's morally corrupt—but that's okay because sleaze sells!

In 1984, Vanessa Williams, reigning Miss America, was asked to resign because she posed nude in an intimate position with another woman. Officials said she had violated the morals clause in her contract. Look at how far we've fallen since the 80's.

Popcorn Generation

Our kids are a right-now generation. They don't have the patience to wait for anything. They have fast cars, instant money, and instant food; they want instant gratification. Everything is electronic.

You can do almost everything online. As a result, nothing is sacred. If you can make your way around a few firewalls, there is no limit to who you can scam. We jumped into this world of automation without knowing how much it would change the way we do business. If you ask a child to balance a checkbook, cut the grass, cook a meal, or wash the laundry, they look at you as if you have spontaneously sprouted a second head. Ask them to get on the computer and find music, download movies that are still playing at the theater, or jailbreak a phone, and it's at your disposal in an instant. As fast as we can build IT security, they can hack into it. We lose millions of dollars every year to these practices. Where is the guidance for these children to do the right thing with this knowledge? Who is teaching them that to whom much is given, much is required? Instead, they hack through system after system, leaving countless victims in their wakes. Do you know what the penalty is for such behavior? A good job! Apparently, the bigger the crook, the greater the pay! Case and point, we have a felon acting as leader of the great US of A.

Justice Is Unjust!

As with everything, there are always exceptions to the rule. Depending on who you are—or if you are the unfortunate individual who becomes an example—life can become a living hell, regardless of success. In 2007, Michael Vick, quarterback for the Atlanta Falcons, was sentenced to twenty-three months in prison for his part in a dogfighting ring. The judge felt that he had not taken full responsibility for his part in the ring.

Now while I agree that killing dogs or any animal, in this manner, is insensitive and criminal, putting Vick in jail did nothing to teach him sensitivity about his activities. Sure it ruined him financially, but with his talent, it only made him fight hard to regain his financial status. Why wasn't he ordered to work in animal shelters and assist in surgeries of animals that had been cruelly abused? He earned good money, and many shelters could have used the monetary assistance. An added bonus would have been the opportunity for him to see the damage done to animals that survive such cruelty.

On February 26, 2013, Trayvon Martin was shot and killed by George Zimmerman after going to the store to buy a soda and a bag of Skittles. Zimmerman was taken to the police station, questioned for five hours, and released because police said they found no evidence to contradict his claim of self-defense. He was still out and free on April 11, 2013, for killing a human being.

An unarmed, seventeen-year-old black boy died because, in Zimmerman's words, he "looked like he was up to no good!" If not for public protest, high-profile celebrities, and the perseverance of the boy's parents, Zimmerman may have never seen the inside of a courtroom. When he was finally charged, old, prejudiced people sent him money to hire the best lawyers money could buy. He was not convicted—and the jurors required a more competent code of conduct from a young boy than they did of the grown man. This man profiled a child, insinuated that blacks always get away with things, disobeyed the dispatcher's order to not follow the boy, and got out of his car with a gun. What really infuriated me was that as Zimmerman sat in the courtroom, looking goofy, he knew it was not his cries for help on the recording of Trayvon Martin's last moments of life. Why would anyone be yelling for help while in possession of a firearm? A human life, the life of a black child, didn't measure up to the life of an animal.

After the verdict, black boys all over the world had to be informed that they could be innocent and die. That there may be a time when they will have to forego their dignity, put their hands up, and lie on the ground as a sign of surrender when they've done absolutely nothing wrong—and they may still die. Even earning a good living that will afford them nice clothes or a top-of-the-line vehicle could cost them their lives. They had to be informed about the importance of character because to protect the guilty party—as long as they are *not* black—lawyers will assassinate a person's character!

The inability to uniform our judicial system produces Susan Smith, Casey Anthony, Scott Peterson, and Josh Powell. It serves as a reminder of the types of parents our children are exposed to. When those with the responsibility to do the right things make criminal decisions, how can we expect children watching these shocking stories to know what is right and what is wrong?

A mother, for whatever twisted reason, gets into her car, children in tow, and drives it into a lake. At the last moment, fear for her own mortality forces her to jump out, leaving her children in the car. She watches as her children drown. She made up a story that she had been carjacked by a black man while her children were in the car, and she made a tearful plea on television to whomever had taken her vehicle not to hurt her children. All the while, she knew right where her children were. Meanwhile, no black man driving a Mazda Protegé within a fifty-mile radius was safe from harassment.

A father-to-be killed his wife while she was pregnant with their first baby. He reported her missing on Christmas Eve, stating that she had disappeared while he was fishing at Berkeley Marina. Four months later, an unborn fetus washed ashore from San Francisco Bay, north of the marina. It was followed by a partial female torso they would later identify as Laci Peterson and her unborn fetus, Connor. Scott Peterson was having an extramarital affair.

A father killed his wife, the mother of their two sons. When her employer called because she had failed to show up for work, he pretended to have no knowledge of her whereabouts. Josh Powell told authorities that when he got up at midnight to take his two young sons camping in the Utah desert in the middle of a snowstorm, his wife was at home asleep in bed. When he became a suspect of Susan Powell's death and his children were taken from him, he became involved in a custody battle with Susan's parents. Though temporary custody was granted to Susan's parents, Powell was awarded court-appointed visits. During one of his supervised visits with the five-year-old and the seven-year-old, he locked the social worker out of the house, attacked the children with a hatchet, and set the house on fire. They all perished in the blaze.

On July 15, 2008, a grandmother contacted 911 because she had not seen her grandchild in thirty-one days. During that time, she had repeatedly asked her daughter to bring two-year-old Caylee to visit her, but she was told one story after another, including that she was with a nanny. It would later be discovered that there was no nanny—and that the person named was not a nanny and had never met Caylee or any member of the Anthony family.

Suspicions mounted when a certified letter affixed to the front door of the family's home from the post office yielded Casey Anthony's car, in a tow yard, smelling of a decomposed body. When the young mother was questioned, she lied. She even told authorities in one of her sordid tales that the nanny had kidnapped Caylee. She showed no concern for her missing child and swore to the police that she was at work at Universal Studios, the same lie she had been telling her parents. When the police asked her to take them to her office, she walked them around Universal Studios for a while before admitting that she had been fired years earlier.

On December 11, 2008, Caylee Anthony's skeletal remains were found wrapped in a blanket inside a trash bag in a wooded area near the family home. Casey was not convicted for the murder of her child and is free, living as if there was never a Caylee while the poor, misguided media clamors to make her rich and famous by being the first to turn her story into a movie.

These are a few pitiful examples of the inhumane parental failures in society.

Morally Challenged

I think the world is in this terrible predicament because of our leadership. Even though the United States has always been a very prejudiced country, it showed enough scruples to put on a face of diversity. I keep hearing that the United States is the greatest country in the world, but I think that belief comes from the perspective of people in countries who have no say in decisions that affect their lives.

Our leaders have the same communist mentality as any other country; they've just found a way to word our bills and laws so that we ultimately vote in favor of the decisions that may have caused a revolt had they passed them without the democratic process. Sometimes they attach a hotly debated bill to a highly favored law so that it is passed without debate. Although this practice is not illegal or unconstitutional, it has become a weapon of choice in our congressional warfare.

I believe the integrity of our leaders needs to change. If a man desires any office, he should first desire good work. He then must be blameless, the husband of one wife or wife of one husband, vigilant, sober of good behavior, given to hospitality, not greedy of filthy lucre but patient; not desiring possessions that belong to someone else and one that rule his own house well, having children under subjection and respectful because if a man can't rule his own house, how can he take care of the world?

This line reminds me of Maureen O'Connor, John Edwards, Anthony Weiner, and Bob Filner to name a few.

Maureen O'Connor, the widow of the founder of Jack-in-the-Box, inherited approximately $50 million after her husband's death. She was the mayor of San Diego and could have lived a very comfortable and satisfying life, but she began gambling. Her game of choice was video poker. She told a CBS reporter that she sometimes lost $100,000 in a day. Going through her fortune like water leaking from a broken faucet, she began selling off properties to raise more money to feed her habit. When that was spent, she raided the charitable foundation set up by her deceased husband, Robert Peterson, of over $2 million.

When the dust settled, she had spent as much as $1 billion and was declared bankrupt. While trying to look contrite, O'Connor had the audacity to tell the CBS reporter that she hoped the San Diego community would forgive her. As is the practice of the United States to enable, they reported that she had found out two years earlier that she had a brain tumor. Her neuropsychologist said it could have contributed to her behavior.

She began gambling in 2001, and the tumor was discovered in 2011. Either there is something wrong with that neuropsychologist or that's a very strange tumor. She should have just owned up to her behavior and admitted that she did exactly what she wanted to do.

John Edwards indulged in an extramarital affair and had a child from the affair. To excuse his actions, he said, "To come from nothing to a successful lawyer, US senator, and national public figure, fed a self-focus, egotism, a narcissism that leads you to believe you can do whatever you want."

This man once ran for president of the American people. Is this what person in position of authority and power believe? How can this be the mentality of a man who wanted to become the leader of our country? What is the measure of a man whose judgment is this obscured?

In 2011 Anthony Weiner, a representative to New York's Ninth District, disgraced himself by sexting, Facebooking, and tweeting inappropriate pictures of himself to countless women. When it became public knowledge, he didn't feel the need to recuse himself from his political position. Democratic leaders pressured him into stepping down. When he finally announced his resignation, he was belligerent to those who had forced him to step down. He said, "I am announcing my resignation from Congress so that my colleagues can get back to work."

He promised to seek mental health treatment. According to his wife of eleven months at the time of his disgrace, he received it. In 2013, while running as a mayoral candidate for New York, it was revealed that the vile sexting did not stop. One year after therapy, he reverted to his former self. He is incapable of comprehending the gravity of his behavior; it is even more disturbing that New Yorkers were even considering accepting him as their mayor at all. This travesty of immorality revealed the mind of Anthony Weiner and the mindless degradation of the American people.

Bob Filner, the former mayor of San Diego, was accused of kissing, touching, and making insensitive sexual comments to women who served under his administration. Despite increasing demands for him to resign, it was never an option for Filner. His attempt to defuse the escalating crisis was to announce that he would undergo two weeks of intensive therapy to improve his behavior toward women. What can two weeks of therapy do for this man who has had seventy years to form this mentality?

As we found out with Weiner, therapy can't teach a tiger to be a zebra. He is a sick, perverted old man, much like a younger, perverse Weiner. Neither should play any roles in the decision-making process of the free world.

There are countless others I could name, but what would that matter? You get the picture. These behaviors are repeated because there is no fear of recrimination for immoral behaviors. If we made examples of everyone who swore to uphold the law and dignity of one's position, these behaviors would crawl back under the rocks they were once hidden under. Many people were killed or paid off to keep secrets, but many resigned under false stories to save face.

Indiscretions have become accepted practices—and that's why there are always new headlines about delusional government officials doing the unthinkable.

CHARLIE BROWN SYNDROME

When I entered the Institute for Children's Literature, I wrote a story about my niece. She found herself in a moral conflict. It was an issue that my sister quickly addressed. She made her daughter aware of the importance of integrity.

When I submitted the story to a publishing company, I was told that the contents had too much parental influence. They would have preferred if the child had arrived at the solution on her own or among her peers. From that experience, I learned that we raise our children like the Charlie Brown cartoons. Charlie Brown and his friends make the decisions governing their own lives because parents are not seen and are rarely heard.

What is the purpose of a parent if children are equipped to make true and accurate decisions? A parent is more than a caretaker of his or her progeny. In my opinion, a parent should have the greatest influence on his or her offspring and in the home. A parent should strive to become a child's role model or someone the child can admire and be proud of.

A parent should make enough of an impression on a child that every toy or food advertisement should not cause a *Nanny 911* emergency. I am a firm believer we must be careful what goes into our children, and it appears that we have become confused about what those things are.

Sesame Street is a PBS program that I watched as a child. It has a character named Oscar the Grouch. Oscar is angry and obnoxious. He is opinionated, unfriendly, and intolerant of all who interrupt him. His character would teach a child that the world has people in it who are not always pleasant. This could be a learning tool or a lesson in building character because it would teach children how to deal with unpleasant people. Carol Parente, executive producer of *Sesame Street*, said that earlier episodes are not suitable for toddlers. Episodes released on DVD come with an adults-only warning. There have also been headlines that declare Oscar and Cookie are dangerous. Their behavior is no longer acceptable on a children's program. They are unpopular and unpleasant, an unacceptable influence. Cookie Monster loves cookies and often eats them with improper etiquette. In the United States, because we have an obesity epidemic, there is talk about making Cookie Monster a vegetable monster so he doesn't influence the eating habits or behaviors of children who watch the show.

What role do Mom and Dad play in decisions of how much or what our children are exposed to? Whose responsibility is it to toe the line of clarity in their homes and in their lives?

We want to alter shows like *Sesame Street*, but I've seen previews of television shows that are popular with teenagers. The shows depict teenagers playing the roles of adults. These shows flaunt teenage pregnancies, lying, cheating, sex, parties with drugs, and plain old dishonesty. The writers, producers, and directors of these shows know that children desire affection and want to fit in. Often devoid of affection, they will accept attention from anyone, even if it's not true affection. Ultimately, these behaviors lead to gang activity or unwanted pregnancies. We glamorize sexuality without responsibility. What real parent would give his or her ten-year-old the keys to a car and expect them to operate it correctly? That is exactly what we are doing when we prematurely introduce our children to adult content. We've saddled our children with grown-up issues before they're equipped to handle them.

When you think about it, there really is little time for children to be children. In fact, we get less than fifteen years. We rob them of those few impressionable years by exposing them to so much that their childhood is gone before they've had time to fully invest in it.

I've heard parents say, "He is eleven years old; I shouldn't have to tell him to do this or that." Sixteen-year-olds are introduced to tasks that exceed their years of experience and are expected to think like adults when they still have teenaged minds. When they perform like the sixteen-year-olds they are, parents act surprised.

Teens do not have the ability to consider the consequences of their actions. Parents know when their children are not ready for a high-performance vehicle, but purchasing it was more about making an impression on their friends than the harm the vehicle could cause. Eighteen-year-olds are confused about some situations they've found themselves in. They are making permanent decisions for temporary situations because we've saddled them with responsibilities that they don't have the skills or knowledge to handle adequately. Every good parent knows that age does not determine maturity.

All of these behaviors are what I call Charlie Brown syndrome. Charlie Brown and his friends consistently make decisions about their own lives. They arrive at many destinations in cars that no adults are seen driving. They plan events, cook meals, and find themselves in impossible situations. Real, live adults would be hard-pressed to get themselves out of some of these situations, but the kids do it all without parental guidance. The only time there is any parental intervention is when they are at school. Questions are answered by a few honks of the teacher's voice.

It was never intended for children to figure life out alone. More parental guidance means fewer confused adolescents. The problem with this idea is the mentality of the parents. They used to lead by example, knowing that it was their job to set the standard of respectability for children to follow. You have only to watch the news to know that adults have no respect for themselves, much less the ability to set a standard of proper conduct for the children in their lives.

Perhaps in Charlie Brown's world, parental guidance is not required in order for children to become well-rounded adults, but sound parental controls are necessary in the real world. They don't need government intervention, laws and legislation, *Super Nanny*, or advice from psychiatrists whose only experiences comes from a classroom of books and studies performed by those before them. Your child's DNA is not in that book, and not every child has problems that require psychological interventions. Sometimes all your children need is a strong hand, direct guidance, and true parental love and concern.

Psychiatrists

All the schooling in the world cannot account for experience. I applaud the intellectual minds that can complete the necessary curriculum to acquire a degree in psychological studies. I believe it can benefit and challenge those who have collectively accumulated the studies that built the profession. The problem with book studies is that you are not in a clinical environment. You are not afforded the ability to feel in your gut or look into the eyes of the people you study. Your only option is to take the information provided (case study) and make a synopsis or diagnosis.

Since real life is much tougher, I believe you should have personal experience in whatever field of study you pursue. My most passionate field is child psychology. If you are going to be a child psychiatrist or psychologist, there should be a residency study portion of the curriculum that requires you to go into the foster care system. For six months, you should take a child into your home to care for them, to parent them, and to teach them. In doing so, you will acquire a more personal experience with the profession that you have chosen as your life's work. This field is not to be taken lightly because the greatest portion of a child's life is yet to be lived. The way a child lives the rest of his or her life could be determined by what was done or not done for them. Parents make all the difference in the world to the outcome of their children's lives in good and bad ways.

Adults, Your Behaviors Are Being Watched

We are constantly dropping our standards in order to accommodate our ever-changing decline in respectability.

We are indulging in deceptive practices; rather than doing the right thing, we hide behind the law. A gentleman I know through an acquaintance worked for a construction company for many years. Jack later acquired a job in an entirely different field. When Jack's wife became ill, he needed extra money, and he offered to do trimming work for friends. His work was so good that friends of friends hired him to do work for them.

One day, Jack went to a gentleman's home at the request of a friend's friend. After Jack completed the work, the gentleman refused to pay him even though the work had been done impeccably. The case ended up in court, and Jack lost because he didn't have a business license. Rather than dwelling on the fact that he did not have a business license, good old-fashioned contract signing and honoring the agreement for payment after services were rendered was not the lesson taught here. No doubt, this was a practice of this man. He had done this to several other unsuspecting people, probably having his home improvement needs done completely free through deceptive practices. His children will learn to use people like he did because they learn by example.

Then we have practices that I can only call justifiable stupidity. For whatever reason, *Rolling Stone* magazine put Dzhokhar Tsarnaev on the front of its July 2013 issue. The magazine usually reserves that place of honor for a deserving rock star, but they decided to place a killer, the bomber of the Boston Marathon, on the cover. Their explanation for this was that the story would deliver. It would show the American people how someone with such a promising future could go so horribly wrong. Who cares? This man and his brother irrevocably changed the lives of countless people with their rampage on American soil. Twelve lives were lost, limbs were amputated at the hands of this man, and *Rolling Stone* thought it befitting to place his face on the front of their magazine? I don't care if he could have been the next pope, that honor does not belong to a murderer. These actions are a constant reminder of the moral decay that is now the mindset of America.

Parents Should Strive to Be Much More

Parents must have the ability to multi-task. They must also remember what it was like to be a child and the emotional rollercoaster that was part of the road to adulthood. When children become a part of your life, those memories should translate to lesson plans. That means being a mediator, especially when there is more than one child involved. Being a *caregiver* requires acquiring some first aid skills, and it means that we become taskmasters, delegating chores designed to introduce the understanding that life is about responsibilities. Our children learn everything from talking to conduct; we are their teachers, but a parent's most important role is being a judge.

Teaching is the quintessential duty that begins from birth, but judging begins when a baby begins to form his or her own personality and mannerisms.

A judge must be able to view a situation from all sides to adequately hand out a sentence. All the facts must be considered—even those we don't want to admit played the largest role in a particular circumstance. When something goes terribly wrong in our children, which seems to be happening more and more every day, we must be prepared to do whatever it takes to make a hypothesis and take immediate action. Sometimes medicine or a psychiatrist is necessary, but those things should be last resorts. Good parenting should be first and foremost.

Children should fear you because that is how respect is taught. They should not fear that you will hurt them or abuse them, but they should fear that you have the power and ability to teach consequences. They should know that for every action, there is an equal and opposite reaction. Good accomplishments reap good rewards. Unpleasant deeds reap unpleasant responses. Parents who fail to do this end up with misguided, entitled, or enabled children.

Parenting is just like any other decision in life. Count up the cost, and see if you're up to the task. There is no turning around once a decision is executed.

HANGING IN THE BALANCE

Balance is a powerful necessity in life. Without balance, things can go terribly awry. That's the way our universe works. There can be no up without down, no in without out, no hot without cold, no light without darkness, no right without wrong, and no heaven without hell.

Some declare they were born gay, some migrated toward it, and others have decided they're gay after living a straight life for forty years. To me, being gay is like deciding one day that I am green. I've always known something was different about me. I don't fit in with whites, blacks, Indians, Asians, or any other race of people. I know I'm green and want to be recognized as such. There are people who look at me funny because I proclaim I'm green. They act as if I've lost my mind, but I know I'm green. I don't want people to treat me wrong because I'm green.

As it turns out, I am not alone. There are other people who say they are green. Some knew from birth, and some arrived at it later in life. What's really powerful is that there are legislators, judges, doctors, teachers, and many more people who are also green. Now the green people have decided to get together to force the world to accept green people the same as non-green people. Green people want to marry, raise children, and have all the privileges of non-green people. Part of the acceptance process is that marriage is redefined to include green people, even though they cannot procreate and their affection is unnatural.

If the way I wrote this story sounds ridiculously offensive to you, that's how ridiculously offensive homosexuality sounds to me. What you should understand though is that even though this is my view of homosexuality, I do not advocate hate. There is never a reason to hate anyone. You can rest assured that I am not, nor have I ever been, nor will I ever be homophobic. I am simply taking a moral stand.

With this in mind, consider that there is a reason why we have males and females. The universe never intended there to be female and female or male and male. There is no balance in that. That balance must begin in a stable, structured environment: the home. The daycare providers and the teachers aren't responsible for providing that environment.

When that structure is amiss, children show up in the judicial system. One of the most commonly asked questions is "where is the father." No matter how masculine a woman is, how close she shaves her head, tattoos her body, wear her pants down, or how much she buffs up, she's still a woman. No matter how much surgery one might receive, or whether one meets the criteria by law that deems a surgically altered person the opposite sex, if you were born with a prostate, penis and testicles, you're male. If you were born with a vagina, ovaries and uterus you're a female. Having those body parts is more than just being born with a piece of hardware (male) or software (female). Each brings genetics that cannot be denied. No matter how masculine a female is, she will never know what it is to be a man or a father, and no matter how feminine a male is, he can never know what it is to be a woman or a mother.

For those who are satisfied with their genders but have a preference for the same sex, there is a great deal of mental confusion and carnality. One must consider that everyone is predisposed to something. Scientists really don't know why a person is an alcoholic, a thief, a rapist, a pedophile, or a genius. In the case of siblings, one can go the way of the parent and the other won't. Whether consciously, subconsciously, or emotionally, the status is a choice triggered by a smell, a touch, a desire, maybe even a memory. Regardless of how you arrived at that conclusion, it's not okay to just label yourself anything without accepting the responsibility for and consequences of that decision. It is illogical to expect everyone to accept a decision you labeled yourself with.

There are those who have lived their entire lives as heterosexuals but change sexual orientations after marriage, giving birth to their children and leading natural lives. How do you wake up one morning and decide that you need to sodomize or be sodomized or that you desire your own genitalia. It is a vile affection to change your natural use into that which is against nature. That is unnatural affection!

Adults, parents, and siblings understand that standing for a position does not mean hating the opposite position.

Rob Portman who previously supported the Defense of Marriage Act and the federal marriage amendment changed his views on marriage between a man and a woman simply because his son came out to him that he is gay. Why would Mr. Portman think that he must change his position on same-sex relationships to love his son? If he really believed in the institution of marriage, there would have been no change of heart; there would have been an enlargement of his heart to encompass his son and his sexual orientation while standing firm on his position. A mother of a drug user, a murderer, or a thief still loves her child and doesn't seek to change the laws that prosecute these acts. Unconditional love doesn't wane in the face of accountability. Hillary Clinton says she supports gay marriage personally and as a matter of policy and law. Why and what does that even mean?

The progression of the acceptance of gay rights will not stop. Right now, churches are not mandated to marry gays, but that's because not every state have passed same-sex marriage laws. Churches don't realize that as soon as most states pass the law that same-sex marriage is no longer same-sex marriage but simply marriage, they will have to marry gay couples or risk facing a hate crime and possibly legal action. Former President Obama said that our journey is not complete until our brothers and sisters are treated like anyone else under the law. As much as I liked President Obama, he can't really believe that. Blacks and women are still not treated equally under the law, and the color of one's skin and gender are not a choice, but homosexuality is.

When we start dabbling into things that were never meant to be tampered with, more and more provisions have to be added to accommodate the offenses. Before we know it, we have so much chaos that each decision seems to undo more of what is right and gives more leverage to what's wrong. We've had to tiptoe around gay issues, and now we've got to decide how to treat transgendered people. Gays took the word gay, which belongs to no one, and claimed it to describe a sexual orientation. If straight people say, "Oh, that's gay," there are serious consequences inflicted upon the user of that phrase. Use it at school, and you may be suspended. They have taken the rainbow, an object that God created as a symbol of peace between man and himself that he would never again destroy the world with water, and claimed it as a symbol of their sexual orientation. The same God they called a liar by going contrary to his intended purpose for them. Our government has decided to rewrite the classifications of the opposite sex, and now you may be sharing the bathroom with a man whose bewildered mind has convinced him that he is and has always been a woman or vice versa.

If you believe that gay relationships are as natural as normal ones, go to the hardware store, purchase two male plugs or two female plugs, and let me know how much power you get.

If You Think You Have a Right . . .

Our world is so filled with hate that to stand for right means persecution or loss in popularity. We've even fooled ourselves into thinking that there is no right or wrong when it comes to matters of the heart. We really need to stand for what we know is right regardless of persecution and put our efforts into rehabilitating minds to understand that having a view of any subject is not a rite of passage to threaten, harass, or demean anyone for it.

That's where bullying originated. Perhaps I don't like you because I classify you as a nerd, you didn't meet my criteria to be a member of the cheer squad, or you gross me out with your pimples. That's why I harass you. All too often, this behavior goes unchecked until some weary child commits suicide because death is more appealing than living another day. I don't think bullies really know why they bully, but their parents know. Real parents even know where the child learned it.

The behaviors of children are a parent's responsibility, but parenting is not taken seriously enough. The presence of reproductive organs doesn't mean you're capable of being a parent. Our society co-signs into these behaviors by vesting way too much interest in Hollywood and the lives of movie stars. The paparazzi continuously overstep boundaries, but the stars' lives that they disrupt are often criticized for retaliating against the invasion of privacy.

So much fanfare was made of the Duchess of Cambridge's impending birth that reporters were paid millions to stand outside St. Mary's Hospital until the new prince or princess was born. We are so enthralled by the lives of celebrities that we don't even know what's going on in our own lives. Tabloid television shows feed this insatiable desire by reporting every detail that they can uncover in the celebrity world. Some bored parents and other adults have nothing better to do than pine for the glamour they see played out on television.

America Is Sick

Jodi Arias shot, stabbed, and slit the throat of her ex-boyfriend because he wanted to get out of the relationship. She went through elaborate schemes to create an alibi that would recuse her as a suspect. Like the Casey Anthony trial, filmmakers wanted to make a movie about her. When did these behaviors go from being considered inhumane and gruesome to being coveted? We have become so desensitized to things that used to be considered repugnant, psychotic, and sadistic.

Is there anyone else who feels that no matter how great a producer, director, or writer someone is, they can't make odious brutality appealing. There is a thin line between creativity and insensitivity, and what our television and movie producers are doing is abhorrent. Glamorizing such detestable stories sends the wrong messages to would-be copycats of such horrific crimes, but it's as if the new generation of media has no filters.

There is something terribly wrong with a society that thrives on the sickness within itself. Anything goes, regardless of the insensitivity of it. America is sick from the neck up, and the sickness is quickly spreading to generation after generation of would-be cognizant human beings. America, the self-proclaimed savior of the world, is spreading its sickness to any nation that seeks shelter from persecution.

Everything Has a Price

Being an American is both a blessing and a curse. The freedom to speak freely and express ourselves in America should come with a disclaimer: you can say what you want, but you'll pay for it, possibly with your life.

One of the saddest stories I have ever heard was about a Giants fan who went to a game against the Dodgers. After leaving the game, he was approached by two men in the parking lot. They began beating him in an unprovoked attack. He was beaten so badly that he lapsed into a coma. The two men escaped in a car driven by a woman with a young child inside.

No human being should have to endure these things for the love of a game or a hobby, and no child should ever have to witness such shameless disregard for human life. The love of the game will change this man's life, and the life of his family, forever. That's just too high a price to pay for the simple pleasures of life.

After many sporting events, especially championships, riots ensue. There are fires, overturned vehicles, and fights. These actions aren't the actions of children or adolescents; adults, parents, and people who hold positions of authority commit them. What happens to these people who take on animalistic tendencies and deny the humanity within to become reminiscent of a beast?

My grandmother used to say if you can't take a punch, don't throw one. My point to that phrase, is what goes around comes around, or you reap what you sow. Maybe you're more familiar with the word karma. It's all the same; whatever you do to someone else will happen to you. Be careful what you dole out because you're most definitely going to get it back.

THE CREDIT AND THE BLAME

At an open house, I looked around the second-grade classroom as we listened to my child's teacher. I noticed a banner over the blackboard that read: *Responsibility means I must accept the credit and the blame.* Perhaps that simple but very profound statement should be written in the Constitution because we are teaching everything except responsibility!

There is too much finger-pointing, but no one is pointing it at themselves. We all must accept our shares of the decomposition of our moral society. As a nation, we have lost our values on so many levels. The value of the dollar is in the toilet. The quality of work and work ethic is at an all-time low.

Chevrolet's slogan used to be: *The pride is back. Born in America... again!* That may have been who we were at one time, but clearly we lack pride in anything that is pure or wholesome. Every time I turn on the television, there is some kind of scandal being reported.

There are self-proclaimed saviors such as Edward Snowden. In a declaration to save the world from the molestation of privacy rights, he decided to download sensitive information on a thumb drive and keep it with him while running from prosecution. How safe do you think that information is in his possession? If the information was not safe from him in a secure facility, how safe does he think it is on his person? Unfortunately, that is the sad reality of the mentality of this generation.

Accountability

The meaning of *accountability* has been losing ground for the past fifty years, and now more than ever. We excuse it away with the same irritation as swatting at pesky insects. We act as if we can't distinguish between imagination and fact. More often than not, the people who are supposed to be the pillars of our society are refusing to accept or teach accountability. We would receive failing grades in several areas if we were students. These behaviors are observed by our children and duplicated like badges of honor.

James Holmes, the cold-blooded, calculating murderer, had the presence of mind to execute a flawlessly cold-hearted plan to shed innocent blood. He booby-trapped his apartment with chemical explosives, turned up the volume on his music to cause a disturbance, and left his apartment. He did so with the intent of inflicting death or serious injuries on the police officers who would enter his apartment when attempts to get him to turn the music down failed.

Knowing this action would dispatch law enforcement and EMT personnel there, he went to the theater looking like the Joker and shot as many people as he could. He parked his car outside one of the emergency exits, went into the theater, and waited until it was almost full of people out for a nice evening with a good movie. He left through the emergency exit, removed the guns from his car, re-entered the theater, and proceeded to shoot human beings as if they were cans. Many lives were lost, but many more would have died if his plan at the apartment had been successful.

His lawyers requested that he undergo a psychological evaluation to see if he was competent to stand trial. How could anyone as calculating as James Holmes be considered incompetent? How does this train of thought move us toward accountability? Put him in prison, and never let him see the light of day again!

These kinds of crimes are courtesy of the lawyers who make up our judicial system. Lawyers are too busy trying to get a win to consider how no one wins when the purpose of getting someone off is to put another mark in the win column or to become famous. If each person they set free would buy a home in their neighborhoods, there might be a lot more criminals behind bars than on the streets.

Our Judicial System

If you have enough money, you can hire the best lawyers. It doesn't matter if you're guilty; the lawyers need only to create reasonable doubt. They studied the law, looking for its inadequacies. They learned how to find loopholes in the law. Good lawyers belong to firms, wear expensive suits and have manicured hair and nails. They drive fine cars and appear to live exemplary lives. They coach their clients on what they should say or whether they should say anything at all. If you look too guilty, like James Holmes did, they will suggest that you may not be competent to stand trial.

People who can't afford to hire lawyers are represented by public defenders. These lawyers don't have the expense accounts, fine cars, or big bucks to impress a jury. Those lawyers have to earn a paycheck.

In the inner city, the crime rate is high. Innocent men, women, and children die every day. Staying inside doesn't exempt a person from loss of life. Gangs are running the streets, and many young boys will never live to become men. It's not lost on adolescents that these murderers are rarely given psychological evaluations to see if they are competent to stand trial. What could have happened in these boys' lives that would cause them to have no regard for human life? What is the difference between one mass shooting and another? Is it money, race, or character traits? How do you explain this distinction to your children?

Perhaps our children can't discern between the right to do something and the rights of others to protest it because the parents can't. We all learn by example. When I was in school, many of my classmates were parents before they had driver's licenses. Sadly enough, this behavior was passed down from the grandmother to the mom to the child, resulting in generations of ignorance.

These children are now grandparents who don't know parenting from basket weaving. They think it is cute to send a seven-year-old to school with large earrings, eye shadow, and provocative clothing. They don't know that maturity is time sensitive and age appropriate. These kids are being set up to become victims of abuse and candidates for behaviors such as histrionic personality disorder (HPD). We must take parenting more seriously to stem the loss of innocence. Our children are experiencing adult issues much too soon!

If we didn't pass laws to prohibit certain behaviors, America wouldn't have the sense to distinguish what is right. This is why we have to pass legislation for things that should be common courtesies. There was a bill before Maryland lawmakers concerning riders of public transportation and profanity. The bill served as a means to make using public transportation more tolerable. People who are reported swearing on public buses could pay fifty-dollar fines.

Several people were livid over the proposal, stating that there are more pressing issues to legislate than cussing. They felt that they should be able to say whatever they want, whenever they want. Another said it was his right to cuss if he wanted to; after all, freedom of speech is an inalienable right in America. People can be as dumb as Billy goats, but they are quick to invoke their First Amendment rights.

Someone on the opposite side of the conversation said his rights were being violated because he was subjected to cussing and swearing on public transportation. Public transportation comes with its own discomforts, including those who swear or disturb the peace, and it is every rider's right to ride in peace.

Though this is not a judicial matter, it serves as another disturbing trend in society.

The AMA has now classified obesity a disease. I expected better than this from such a prestigious group of professionals. I can agree that obesity *causes* diseases. I will even agree that an underlying condition may cause obesity, but a person who eats enough to weigh six hundred pounds does not have a disease. He or she lacks discipline and self-control. When we assign medical terms to irresponsible behaviors, we enable and create people who refuse to exercise self-control. Empathy and sympathy have their places, but feeling sorry for a nation that refuses to accept responsibility for its own actions is unacceptable!

The Grass Is Always Greener

America has a hero complex. Whenever there is a crisis or civil unrest in another country, we put on tights and a cape and fly off to save the day. We police the world by asserting our opinions and holding wrongdoers accountable. How can a country with a military that assaults its female soldiers, and whose political leaders harass women, judge the wrongdoings of others? We do not do enough for veterans who have done multiple tours of duty when they return home broken and mentally exhausted.

Besides a lack of honor, we are too impressionable to police any other nation. We changed our school curriculum to try to compete with foreign countries. Our children can't even have recess like the days of old. We equate less playing with more learning. We think cramming more economics will make us like Chileans and Brazilians. We don't learn like those countries, and we don't have the discipline of Hong Kong, Portugal, or Poland. The curriculum isn't why we can't compete. The problem is the parents and the attitudes of the educators. Parents don't expect excellence, and educators don't encourage achievement. Having to address so many behavioral issues makes education secondary in the classroom. The beginning of the road to excellence begins at home.

We try to impress naturalized citizens to the point of denying ourselves. Our history celebrates tradition and days of observance. Why do we allow foreigners to influence our traditions. We can't put up nativity scenes at Christmastime or say "Merry Christmas" because we don't want to offend those who feel Christ is being forced on them. I can tell you unequivocally that Americans can't enter other countries and change their religious orientations or rituals.

Where America should have been a hero was to black Americans. Maybe the reason America was so quiet during the holocaust was because it didn't want to have to explain why they had a sect of people that they treated with as much disregard as Hitler did the Jews. If you review history, you'll see that Americans have lacked sensitivity. Racism ruled the South and still lives there. Racists killed little girls and boys because of the color of their skin. Authorities knew the perpetrators of these crimes, but they turned their heads because it was an accepted practice. There would be no atonement for those lost lives, and there was no one to call America to the seat of retribution. There would be no prosecution for these crimes, and the perpetrators would go on to live full lives and die surrounded by the love of family and friends.

Even today, Americans exhibit behaviors that display a lack of sensitivity and responsibility for the elderly. Most employers know that the kind of money it would take for people to retire and live comfortably far exceeds the amount they could ever hope to pay into a 401(k). There are fees attached to the plans, and most Americans are poor investors. Most have no idea how much they will need to retire, and employers don't tell them because it's a very dismal outlook unless you reach your expiration date before your funds expire. Those who have helped themselves to investment funds and scammed people out of their retirement in Ponzi schemes and other tactics complicate the process. Millions will end up with only Social Security during retirement. All these examples exhibit a lack of self-examination and recrimination. The work should begin here and not in other countries.

Americans are outraged by injustices and disrespect in other countries, but there is so much of it right here at home. People go on missions to third-world countries and risk their lives to right a wrong. Who will go on a mission to save the unfortunate in American ghettos?

There is no justice for those in the wrong social circles. The nation is too divided to save itself. How do we proudly wear the big Superman logo on our chests when we're as broken as the world we police?

WE SHOULD LEAD BY EXAMPLE

Opinions are like noses; everyone has one. Unfortunately, opinions have taken a seat in society that they haven't earned.

In an interview with Charlie Rose, Dick Cheney criticized President Obama's choices for his cabinet. He said the president had a second-rate team and he conveyed no care for John Kerry but with respect to Chuck Hegel and John Brennan, he said, "That's all the president." The president chooses the people he wants around him and basically chooses people who won't argue with him. Cheney added that he was concerned with what he saw. He believed that President Obama chose Chuck Hegel, a Republican, to foil what he wanted to do to the Defense Department.

Why should anyone care what he thinks? Why did the media think he was qualified to weigh in on this administration? Most young adults have no idea who Dick Cheney was. He had little to no input in the first four years as vice president and had to practically threaten President Bush in his second term to let him do something or let him go.

At the time, Cheney was CEO of Halliburton, a company with very questionable practices, including significant overbilling and an association with Kellogg, Brown, and Root (KBR). Halliburton was accused of overcharging the Pentagon and the military. His company was frivolous in its billing of goods and services and careless in its responsibility for the equipment it was liable for. They were accused of charging subcontractors a hundred dollars for a fifteen-pound bag of laundered clothes and left an $85,000 truck by the roadside for simple maintenance issues, including a flat tire.

KBR, a subsidiary of Halliburton, was accused of political corruptions, sexual assault and abuse, and human trafficking. In

2003, KBR was caught charging the US Army $1.59 per gallon of imported oil from Kuwait for which it had paid 70 cents per gallon. Even though Cheney retired from Halliburton at a package worth $33.7 million and was forced to sell stock worth $30 million, he was still receiving deferred income of 433,000 in stock options in 2007. During much of his vice presidency he was ill and MIA. Now, with all the grandeur his silver spoon can muster, he wants to weigh in on another administration? Please!!!

John Hagee, who was senior pastor of Cornerstone Church in San Antonio, stated in one of his rambling sermons that God will hold America responsible for electing a president who supports men marrying men. He claimed that we have made a choice and are going to pay the consequences for our choices.

I really liked President Obama, but I do not share his support of gay rights. However, he has done what every president before him has done! He's made some questionable decisions, but we have had a president that historians believed was a gay pedophile and presidents who had affairs. America has signed and broken treaties. We've passed legislation to take prayers out of schools, hung black men from trees, and set them on fire while placing their children in chicken coops to watch them burn. White Americans bought slaves and crept out of bed from white wives to rape black female slaves simply because they could and then denied the children born out of their acts. America took good land from Indians and forced them to live on reservations.

George Wallace blocked segregation at the University of Alabama by standing in a doorway to prevent two black students from attending. He was responsible for ordering the brutal attack on a civil rights march over the Pettus Bridge, creating the infamous Bloody Sunday. These transgressions are only a tiny portion of the choices Americans have made. Does Pastor Hagee believe that electing a president who supports gay rights is the only choice that America is going to have to pay for?

When Jeremiah Wright, pastor of Trinity United Church of Christ, whom President Obama had attended the church of, went off on a tangent about God damning America for among other things, the U.S Government using HIV as a means of genocide against people of color, everyone was incensed over his rhetoric. Pastor Hagee's comment met with little pessimism. Each of these people have expressed strong opinion but without facts that's all it is.

These people are in positions that are supposed to set examples of leadership. They are in the public eye and have the ability to sway opinions. Knowing this, they should be very careful about the lives they lead. It's not their words that people see—it's their actions.

Our children are watching how the adults in their lives handle controversy. It has to be tough trying to teach exemplary leadership when greed appears to be the greater motivator.

America has allowed greed to dictate common sense. Politicians have become so engrossed in the convenience that monetary wealth can afford that they will legalize anything to get a dollar, regardless of how questionable it is. As if there aren't enough accidents involving teen drivers, the intense desire for material wealth is about to make it worse. Some teens text while driving, indulge in underage drinking while driving, and race up and down our highways, endangering their lives and the lives of others.

Maryland and a few other states must feel like they can handle more death and carnage since they legalized marijuana for recreational purposes. How can we expect children to make good choices if this is an example of leadership? Are we really that hard up for money that we would legalize marijuana just so we can tax it? Who is liable when more accidents is the result of such stupidity? Adults should know that they can't make laws with total abandonment. Someone must be a respectable authority.

When we exercise true parenting, we establish respectable authority and we become part of an exclusive club: the club of stewardship. This may sound like a total contradiction, but even though parents must show leadership, they also must be ready to serve, manage the needs of the household, and accept responsibility for safeguarding its value. The members of this club can have a positive impact on our jobs, our churches, and our homes, which indirectly impacts the world.

Unfortunately, government officials don't realize the greatest leadership is servitude, which is evident in the lack of respectability, integrity, and morality displayed since electing and re-electing our current president. I believe with all my heart that re-electing Donald Trump as our president was driven by the hatred America still feels for people of color. During Obama's presidency, speaker Boehner was at the helm of the congressional party that failed the American people. Rather than working as a unit to make decisions that would move our country forward, they blocked efforts and pointed fingers.

Elected officials used all kinds of excuses to explain why they couldn't work with former President Obama. All the while, trying to convince the American people that it had nothing to do with his race and everything to do with irreconcilable differences. The real reason was prejudice, and there was a real fear that, with bipartisan support, a black president could accomplish much of what past administrations had been unsuccessful at achieving. There was no way our legislators were going to let that happen. Now that Obama is no longer our president, the affordable care act and even some of our constitution is being thrown out with the current administration.

Because discrimination is illegal, it has many names which makes it difficult to prove. Prejudice is a form of discrimination, but it is not against the law. I am convinced that prejudice is alive and well and living in America. Before President Obama was elected, words like *fiscal cliff* or *sequester* were unheard of.

When Mitch McConnell said his top priority was to make Barack Obama a one-term president, many of his constituents openly agreed. Others quietly did their parts to sway public opinion away from him.

These aforementioned issues serve as reminders that there is more than one way to discriminate.

Parents, you have an obligation to talk to your children. Sit down with them when events in our world are wrong because the issues they see now will someday be their issues. Be honest about what is happening and how it happened. Be sincere about the law, and let them know that regardless to how many laws there are, someone always falls through the cracks. Make them realize that they don't have to be willing victims. Make sure they understand that there are all kinds of leaders, and they don't have to be world leaders to make a difference. They can be leaders in their jobs, in their homes, and in their communities.

Whether a migrant worker in a field or the president of the United States, they have a moral obligation to be the best leaders they can be. Tell them that life isn't always fair. Explain that how they handle what happens to them is more important than what happens to them. Let them know they always have choices. Make sure they know the choices they make can change the world. Teach them what to do with grief, hurt, pain, and fear; their responses to those emotions and any decisions they make can be worthy of paying it forward.

Pay It Forward

The good things that happen in our world usually begin with a simple act of kindness. Someone has a thought about doing something good to help a person or a group and shares it with a friend. Before long, a group of good-hearted people bands together to make someone's life a little more bearable.

Raising children takes money and times get hard now and then. When someone buys you lunch or discretely places a few dollars in your hand to tide you over, realize that you won't always be down. When times are better for you, remember the kindness bestowed upon you. If you're in a grocery store and the person in front of you is short by a dollar or two, it's a show of humanity to pay it for them. If you are ever the beneficiary of a good deed, pay it forward. Acts of charity display the best of human decency. We can be no stronger than the weakest American. We need to work to become the America I know we can be.

Our Fathers Are AWOL

We can become a better America by understanding the importance of our individual roles. Thank God for mothers who have been invaluable in their children's lives, but fatherhood is not mom's role.

Understudies are playing the roles of our fathers because fathers have walked away from their responsibilities. Moms are thankful for uncles, brothers, cousins, and pop-pops who take your sons fishing, to the ball field to throw the ball around, or to the movie with some of his friends, but its dad's responsibility to have the greatest influence on his child.

Many young boys and girls are being raised by stepfathers—or no fathers at all—while the dad has moved on to another relationship. The new woman in his life has children by another dad, but neither dad is taking care of his responsibility. I will state for the record that I have nothing against stepfathers. I was raised by the best non-biological father in the world. He helped me become the human being I am, and his impact in my life has been immeasurable. If my biological father understood the impact he could have had on my life and had placed the needs of his children above his own selfish desires, he would be able to claim bragging rights for producing one of the best contributors to mankind in America.

Fathers, you must know how important your role is in your children's lives. It's hard enough to raise one child and give your time and monetary support. Some men have many children and are raising none. Some men wouldn't give monetary support if the courts had not ordered them to do so.

Men should not be so ruled by testosterone that a couple of their children are born to different women in the same month. If they can't handle the responsibility, they should wrap it up. Women, under some insurance plans, birth control is free. Please exercise your right and use it. If the fathers who stay could teach their successes to the next fathers, there would be the potential to pay it forward until every child in America has a dad at home.

Charitable Contributors

What we lack in one area, we make up in another. Though we lack men who will accept the responsibility of being a father, there is an inherit kindness in our world for the innocent and victims who have suffered in a disaster.

When Haiti suffered an earthquake in 2010, people sent millions of dollars in humanitarian aid. People from all over the world sent food, and doctors came from all over the world to lend a hand, but Haiti has still not been built back as it should have been.

When Hurricane Katrina struck New Orleans in 2005, the levees were breached, causing widespread flooding and death. The best of our world came through in the form of millions in human kindness.

Unfortunately, for every good intention there are ten bad ones. Opportunists tarnished the generosity by violating the rules of common dignity. The scamming of people who had already suffered such devastating losses in the form of life and bare essentials was shameful. The programs put in place were supposedly designed to assist the affected residents, but they were shabby and unsecured. It was handled with such mismanagement that the reconstruction process was profitable for everyone except the victims. FEMA, Halliburton, and the Shaw Group could have done better hiring subcontractors after winning no-bid contracts. There was no excuse for the way that disaster was handled. Many walked away with fat pockets; when the dust settled, the residents still had no home to return to.

America is too intelligent to have made those mistakes in New Orleans. They know protocol and how to distribute funds. This is another example of how senseless failures hurt those who suffer the most.

THE HOUSE THAT JACK BUILT

Our lives begin with the history of our parents' lives. Every decision they made was a direct result of their experiences and impacted our lives through influence or persuasion. As we live, we also build our lives based upon personal victories and failures. They keep us inside the box, give us enough confidence to step outside the box, or propel us toward limitless possibilities. "The House that Jack Built" is a term that I use to define the outcome of life as a result of choices made.

When I was young, one of the ladies who attended our church became fearful of moving water because her son drowned in a lake one hot summer day. As a result, her grandchildren were not allowed in the ocean or any other body of water; even pools scared her to death. She built a house of fear that spilled over into the lives of her other children and their children.

One year, there was a very popular doll that my children showed me while we were shopping for school supplies. Whenever we would go school shopping, they always wanted to go through the toy section to show me what they wanted for Christmas. When I went back to purchase the doll, they were out of the color I wanted. I went to several stores and finally ended up at a Toys "R" Us. There, the doll cost more than I wanted to pay, but since my girls hadn't acted out when my answer to some of their requests were no, I wanted to reward their behavior.

Christmas was always a good time to remind them about all the good they did. When I asked one of the employees if the store had the dolls, he said yes. Even though the store was crowded, he quickly took me to where the dolls were. Alas, they too had sold out of the color I sought. I made a comment to him about other colors of the popular doll and was told that this particular color sold out quickly.

Economics 101 taught me the meaning of supply and demand. If that color always sells out, the store should stock more of it unless it was using a bait-and-switch tactic. I looked at him and wondered if it would matter to him if this child lovingly carried a black doll. When I told a friend that I was having a difficult time finding the doll in the color I wanted, it sparked a debate. I made a point of purchasing dolls that were the same color as my children. To do anything less sent the wrong message. I felt, and still feel, that they can relate to and identify with a doll that reflects themselves. I believed it inspired a strong self-image. That is the house I built that was colored by my past.

Pretend your life is like building a house. While building a home, the foundation rests on footers. Next comes the framing and flooring. After framing and roofing, close in the structure, and install your doors, windows, siding, and shingles. If you don't think about the substance of your decisions and choose substandard products (or make a thoughtless decision) rather than using the very best cement to pour your footers, how will your foundation (the next decision you make) sit on top of an inferior footer? Using the same substandard cement for the blocks of your foundation (more bad decisions) will further serve to build a shoddy structure (life).

By the time you get to the roof, doors and windows (the protector of its contents) and the transparent walls that allow the passage of light (eyes to the soul), the fit will be imperfect and inferior. In such a structure, how productive can life be? The style, size, and condition of the house you build (the life you live) depend upon your thought process, considerations of consequences, and responsibility of life lessons.

Many of us live in dilapidated houses with no hope of renovations simply because we made decisions that were easy and devoid of liability. Each generation finds it easier and easier to continue this trend because accountability is no longer a requirement.

Usually, people who make a mess of their lives live to pass it on to their children and act as if they have no idea how they got in some terrible predicament in their lives. There was a show called *Nanny 911*, and then *Supernanny*. The purpose of these shows was to assist parents in dealing with their uncontrollable children. I'm confused by the fact that the child is the product of both parents, but they have become afraid of the child in three years.

You have to hide every imaginable thing that can be used as a weapon. You have been spit on from your face to your shoes because you've begun saying no to a child you've only said yes to since he or she was old enough to know the difference between yes and no. You didn't think anything so darned adorable could become so unmanageable, all because no boundaries were ever established. Your handsome little son now has purple hair, wears black lipstick, and has piercings from his eyebrow to his belly button—and God knows where else. He wears black fingernail polish and has so many tattoos that there is no visible skin unmarked. When some years later, his face is plastered on the evening news for some unimaginable act of violence, you are perplexed!

Perhaps you have a child who appears to be a little quiet, somewhat withdrawn, or sometimes quite moody, but he or she is a good kid for the most part. These kids are later described by all who knew them as loners, a little creepy, and friendless. They were rarely seen talking to anyone. Did anyone really know what was going on with the quiet, withdrawn child? Did the parents investigate by checking the child's room, dropping by the school from time to time, or simply communicating with him or her? Did they justify these behaviors with the idea that some children are just like that?

The builders of this life haven't considered any possible consequences. They don't realize how negligence can affect more than just the contractor and the homeowner. These callous decisions affect society. It is important that every aspect of this house is built specifically to accommodate the needs of the inhabitants.

This is the house that America has built. The footers bear the weight of the structure. Its purpose is to prepare the ground for receiving the foundation. The intent was for it to hold all the treasures our lives would afford us, but it was poured with inferior cement.

The foundation is the basis of our being; it is our purpose. The servitude of our structure was meant to support us as we built higher and higher upon ourselves. It was meant to be a little better every level, but we lost the objective. We have been selfish and neglectful. We have been disdainful and contemptuous; our purpose lost.

The floor is our conscious and the awareness of our structure. Its purpose complements our existence with grace and lets us live with virtue. Be the light of our world. Enforce the duties set before us with pride. Failed! The head has become the tail, the laughingstock of the world; our value is depleted. Our denial is evident in our distorted views of ourselves. We are certain that we are still head of the free world. Everyone except us knows that we are no longer.

The doors are integrity, protecting our value. Even in our ignorance, we knew the difference between corruptible and incorruptible. We know that no matter how many locks we put on the door, it cannot keep out what the homeowner allows in. We made bad choices and tried to move forward even as we became aware of our indiscretions. As homeowners, we struggled with change, but our integrity should have won out in the end. Somewhere between the awareness of our ignorance and the realization of our cunningness, we lost the superiority that should have made us sound. As a result, we opened up to lust of the flesh, temptation to the eyes, and the pride of life. Therein, we lost what was supposed to have been our excellence.

The windows are our judicial system. The supreme law is supposed to let in the light of goodness and justice. We began with injustices against people of color. Laws were written that excluded people because they were considered property. Time allowed the windows to be opened, and the winds of change blew in. We were on the right track when we created the Declaration of Independence. "We hold these truths to be self-evident, that all men are created equal." Sadly not only did it fail to catch on, it regressed and took with it the mechanism to rule without bias. The windows are boarded up, and the inhabitants are dying.

The roof is the protector of the contents it covers. We have always known right from wrong. Our existence was patterned after that knowledge, but as wrong crept into our house, we justified it in the name of equality. The sheer volume of it began to punch holes in the roof. Now our standard of conduct has let anything and everything in and has infected the inhabitants like *Mycobacterium marinum*. The infection begins when a weak spot is found in the protector's defense, allowing the infection to grow until the body becomes septic. The contents are left defenseless and are destroyed eventually.

This is America's house. It was confused, it chose oblivion over perception, and it lacked strength. Its lackadaisical attitude created an environment of total chaos and is moving quickly to self-destruction.

America's house was built with careless decisions, thoughtless behaviors, and a blatant disregard for the responsibilities it was obligated to acquire as the contractor for the lives inside it. Now the structure whose blueprint promised a house of grandeur has missed its potential. There is no hope for this house.

SUMMARY

Arguably America has maintained its position in the minds of many as the best country in the world, but America began under questionable circumstances. Once we began taking what was not ours, we developed a "gimme" attitude. Throughout our history, we had opportunities to correct wrongs made along the way, but we justified our moral indiscretions and kept moving in the wrong direction.

America once called itself the "Great American Melting Pot," but it has become a big old trashcan, picking up trash from within and without and calling it freedom. We're breeding unnatural mannerisms and have given our children front-row seats with notebooks and pencils to observe the improprieties. We don't think giving children drugs to change their sexes just because they say they're transgendered is utterly ridiculous, and we believe we have a right to redefine sexual orientation. Somewhere in our psyche, we've forgotten that our sexuality is hardwired to our origin. Your sexual orientation is by design not by mind. No amount of surgery can change the body when it is reduced to bones; anatomy will not lie.

We have become arrogant enough to go into other countries to dictate how they should conduct themselves. Our egotism makes us believe that countries that take hard-line stances against any behaviors they feel will ultimately infest their citizens, is ludicrous and unconstitutional. We refuse to recognize that it is not wrong for other countries to set their own standards for moral conduct and expect the general population to conduct themselves accordingly.

We have kicked holes in the Constitution and the judicial system and won countless hollow victories because we have forgotten how to empathize without mitigating.

Foolishness has taken over common sense so that the love of money or notoriety trumps common decency.

Our definition of justice is to replace issues that require playing the hand you were dealt with rationalization.

We become downright indignant when it comes to monetary issues that could affect our legacies. We loudly protest decisions that we feel will affect our children and our children's children, but when it comes to moral conduct, it's live and let live.

Lawyers are using their profession to manipulate people. Religious leaders are trying to redefine the Bible to suit people rather than teaching people to conform to the Bible.

Teachers are using their positions to abuse the trust granted them by doing unthinkable things to our children. Parents are missing the mark of accountability and responsibility in the moral and principle development of children.

Doctors are performing surgeries because people have enough money to pay for the procedures rather than using their beautiful minds to improve humanity. If doctors want to do their jobs, they'll stop changing the bodies and start fixing the minds.

The Creator of the universe will hold each person responsible for his or her share in the moral, legal, ethical, and civil degradation of our civilization.

If I could use one more example of how disorganized our world has become, I would say it looks as if a bomb has gone off, leaving our world in disarray. Instead of trying to clean up the mess, we sat down in the middle of it and have begun to set up house.

We've invented things that are killing us, from plastic to batteries. The ground is contaminated, and the food supply is unsafe. Pharmaceutical companies are making medicines that treat one ailment while creating another. There is so much good we can do to improve our world, but we foolishly chase after frivolous projects that offer short-term fixes and instant gratification.

Our concepts are more ridiculous than trying to harness the wind. While we chase impossible feats, movie stars, video games, television, football players and circumstances are influencing our children. It's time to start doing the best we can for them and stop chasing the wind; our children are easier to catch!

MESSAGE TO PARENTS

Once upon a time, there was a great farmer who was known throughout the world. So great was his reputation that to be considered one of his farmers was among the highest of honors. Every so often, he would choose candidates to grow his seeds. The good thing about the farmer was that he randomly chose his potential growers. Past indiscretions played no part in his decision, and he did not judge.

Once he chose his farmers, he gave each of them a certain number of seeds. The great farmer's seeds were special because none had the same attributes, but each contained the ability to achieve limitless possibilities. The job of the chosen farmers was to nurture and extract the greatest potential from the seeds. In addition to fame and achievement, the winner of the contest would receive knowledge, accolades, and a lifetime of rewards and benefits.

Due to the diversity of farmers, some seeds were disseminated in areas that had not seen water for years. Some went to cement jungles where little ground was available. Others went to where the land was abundant but not always fertile or where the ground was limited but of good quality. Regardless the region, the great farmer knew that those he had chosen were capable of producing a good crop in any circumstances.

Now replace the seed with children. The moral of the story is that the environment will never be perfect. There will always be circumstances and situations that have the potential to challenge your efforts and thwart your success. It should not be lost on you, what a privilege it is to be given the opportunity to instill in a child everything they need to become one so great that by his very life you will inherit a lifetime of honor and rewards. This is what God intends when he allows you to become parents.

MESSAGE TO THE CHILDREN

You have a charge to keep. Being children does not exempt you from the responsibility of making good decisions. Whether you came from a good background or one that is not so good, you have a choice in the outcome of your life. You can take a virtual stance in the path you find yourself on and come out of any situation. Will it always be easy? Absolutely not, but I'm certain it will be worth it.

The road from adolescence to adulthood is rife with pits, peaks, and valleys. There will be great moments and there will be horrible ones, but they are only moments! Don't be so quick to make irreversible decisions. Remember that the things most worth fighting for are the hardest to achieve. Fight hard to reach the point where you reap the rewards of your life's work.

When you take shortcuts in life, you are living a life of mediocrity. It's your choice to accept the constructive criticism and chastisement that it will take to make you a productive adult. The right decisions will enable you to obtain the very most out of life. Life has a way of teaching any lessons you evaded as a child in much harsher ways as an adult. Why not learn it the first time around?

I wish I could promise you that life doesn't have tragic moments, and I wish I could say that bad things don't happen to good people, but I can't. I can say that you are a nation of conquerors and overcomers. Take the negative things in life and turn them into positive resources for those who will come after you.

Take the time to enjoy your life; once it's gone, you can never get it back. Live to have experiences that you will not regret. Make decisions that will not follow you to your grave. Above all, accept responsibility for your decisions.

Treat people the way you want them to treat you.

Smile often.

Laugh out loud.

Be good to your parents.

Remember that every morning is a new opportunity to get it right.

Live with such vigor that when you close your eyes for the last time, people will be glad they got to know you rather than being glad you're gone!

TO THE NEWTOWN COMMUNITY

First of all, please accept my sincerest heartfelt condolences. On December 14 2012, as "Breaking News" scrolled across my television screen. Never in my wildest imagination would I have thought it could be something so horrific. My heart immediately went out to the Sandy Hook community.

Who would have ever thought that after all you've gone through, you would have to wage a battle to protect future lives from becoming victims of gun violence. I commend you for your endurance in the face of such an unimaginable tragedy. I wonder how you found the strength and courage to be a David facing a giant, knowing it would be an uphill battle.

My chest swelled with pride for you as you went before the giant with the hurt and memories of loved ones lost, fighting for the safety and protection that should be afforded every innocent life.

When I think of my own town and the various children I come into contact with, I think about Noah, Ben, Jessie, Dylan, and the twenty-two other precious lives lost. Don't give up. I know that waking up without your children each day is a harsh reality, even now. As we continue to fight for vindication, we will remember that it may take some time, but that giant must fall.

Our prayers are with you.

TO THE PARENTS OF TRAYVON MARTIN

Mr. Martin and Ms. Fulton, there are no words that can express the hurt you have suffered. I am so sorry for your loss. I am appalled by the outcome of the trial, but I will not waste words on what most of the world knows was a travesty of justice. I prefer to use my words to encourage the two of you.

I watched you keep your dignity and pride throughout the most arduous circumstances. I admired your strength even while you struggled to contain your grief, and I prayed for you as the verdict was announced. No parent should have to bury a child, but having to do so because of such a senseless act and then deny yourself the anger that usually accompanies this kind of grief must have taken an astronomical amount of self-control and dignity. When you said your faith is what kept you, I knew that your faith in God had to be unshakable, even in the face of what must felt like an insurmountable challenge.

Do not waver! You'll have some good days, and you'll have some not-so-good days, but don't stop fighting. Therein lays your strength. Keep your eyes on God, your hands in his hands, and your mind on Jesus. He will keep you in perfect peace, a peace that passeth all understanding.

Remember the Word of God never returns to him void. With that in mind, remember Galatians 6:7: "Be not deceived, God is not mocked for whatsoever a man sow, that shall he also reap." God will be with you when you think you can stand no more, just know he will never leave you nor forsake you. God bless.

www.ingramcontent.com/pod-product-compliance
Lightning Source LLC
LaVergne TN
LVHW052003060526
838201LV00059B/3803